A VOYAGE IN VERSE

Edited by

Neil C Day

First published in Great Britain in 2001 by
ANCHOR BOOKS
Remus House,
Coltsfoot Drive,
Peterborough, PE2 9JX
Telephone (01733) 898102

HB ISBN 1 85930 992 5
SB ISBN 1 85930 997 6

FOREWORD

This special anthology offers a unique collection of poetic expressions and inspirations on life and the world around us. Featuring accessible poems that can be enjoyed by all, we are sure that there is something here for everyone. Each poem is communicated across the barriers and helps develop that vital bond between reader and author.

Anyone who ventures within these pages will be treated to a host of delightful and engaging poems delivered in earnest from the poetic heart.

Read on and enjoy the unique gift of poetry at its best.

Neil Day
Editor

CONTENTS

I Survived	J L Kelly	1
Averse, Or Worse	P Elias	2
Sums Without Total	John Amsden	3
Decisions, Decisions	Jonathan Covington	4
School Holidays	A J Renyard	5
Who Is She?	Irene Hart	6
Where?	Matthew L Burns	8
Sleep Divine	Gillian Mullett	9
Ballad To Robin Hood	Christine Brown	10
Gone Away?	Keith Allison	12
The Ballad Of Moonshine Valley	Alma Montgomery Frank	13
The Ballad Of Alferd Packer	Ray Smart	14
Today	Mabel Helen Underwood	16
Indian Wedding	Joyce Walker	17
The Very Best Yet	Sally Anne Hayes	18
Waiting	Pam Redmond	19
Obsession	Hilary Dominy	20
Sudden Pain	Kathleen M Hatton	21
The Risen Sunlight	Dalsie Mullings	22
So Happy	S Mullinger	23
Seagoing Villanelle!	R Bissett	24
Reflections	Winifred Lund	25
Broken Heart	Margarette L Damsell	26
Love?	Marie O'Driscoll	27
Rag Man	Joan Egan	28
To Stand And Stare	Diana Momber	29
Green Shoots	Joyce Hockley	30
Pit Closure	Colin Palfrey	31
Sentence	P J Harris	32
As Watcher Longs	S Pete Robson	33
Communication Is A Must	Barbara Jermyn	34
Deny It?	Deborah Montague	35
Winter White	Joan E Blissett	36
All Is Gone Away	June Clare	37
Two Haiku	Gillian Fisher	38

Faith	Leslie Holgate	39
Haiku	John Clarke	40
Autumn Seeds	Danny Coleman	41
Natural Pleasure	Kate Laity	42
Alone In The Crowd	Millicent Coleman	43
Time	Margaret Ballard	44
Gibberish	Sarah Eden	45
Departure	H D Hensman	46
Haiku	Janet Miller	47
Tanka	B Holmes	48
Haiku	Terry Daley	49
Four Seasons	Catriona Barville	50
Nowhere Compromising	Rowland Warambwa	51
Inexplicably Entwined	Ann G Wallace	52
Tanka	Vicky Stevens	53
Haiku: Hitchin	Richard George	54
Thinkers	Hugh Jackson	55
Nature's Balm	F L Brain	56
Sweet Vision - A Tanka Sequence	Dan Pugh	57
Street Lamp	Jonathan Goodwin	58
An Autumn Wind	Helen Marshall	59
Inspiration	A E Ritzkowski	60
Heat	C Griffiths	61
In All It Lies	Sid 'de'Knees	62
Nature's Artist	Sonia Riggs	63
Tanka	Hilary Jill Robson	64
Awakening	Patricia Batstone	65
Haiku/Tanka	Glenna Welsh	66
Comeliness And Calm	John P Evans	67
Tanka Of Life	Martin Mooney	68
Armistice, Resistance Ended (Tanka Poem)	Loré Föst	69
Commitment	Albert Boddison	70
First Sight Of Snow	M Barnes	71
Tanka	Chris Hatherall	72
What Is A Tanka?	Ken Price	73
Cross	Peter Davies	74

Shades Of Life	Susan Seward	75
In A Non-Holding Pattern	Francis McFaul	76
First Flight	Celia G Thomas	77
Ending	Sheila E Harvey	78
Seasons	Maureen Cassidy	79
Whisky	Robbie Innes	80
God Loves Todays	Roger Brooks	81
Ballad Of Poetry Waste	Colin Allsop	82
Countryside Church Treasury	James Leonard Clough	83
Commissionaire	John McPartlin	84
Forever Young	Paul O'Boyle	85
The Old Thatch	John Cook	86
Reflections	Oliver Eadie	87
Bombs And Bullets	R E Humphrey	88
Eden - Cornwall 2001	Pat Heppel	89
Now And Then	Tom Sawyer	90
Retaining Wall	Walter Blacklaw	91
The Exile	Joan E Blissett	92
His Love	F R Pavitt	93
Wonders Of The World	Claire Victoria Hale	94
Who's There?	Sandra Wolfe	95
Sonnet For Marie	Edmund Saint George Mooney	96
The Pleasure Beach	Martin Howard	97
Fools Rush In . . .	Cherry	98
Freedom	Judith Thomas	99
'Ecstasy' - Why? (A Sonnet)	Mick Nash	100
Magpie	Caroline Kemp	101
Nursery Rhymes (With Gravity)	Norma Meadows	102
The Portrait Painter	M MacDonald-Murray	103
Sonnet For Michael	Ute Elliott	104
Golden Afternoon	Kathleen M Scatchard	105

I Survived

I survived the tangled waves of life,
I rode them all and won,

I know it was not made easy,
but who said life was fun?

Through the tangles of my emotions
I see more clearly now,

Forgetting all the whys and wheres
For whose done that and how,

Quite often on a starry night,
when God was not around

I'd hear him talk to me, to let me know,
all I'd lost, was found,

Even in my moments and my doubts
through fear and despair

I'd like to think you're with me God,
to love me and to care.

J L Kelly

AVERSE, OR WORSE

I'm quicker by seamail
Than I am by email.

The last time I emailed a friend
Thrice I tried a message to send
But instead each time I did delete
My message before deciding I would quit.

Besides, I find I much prefer
A picture postcard than to err.

Too often I end up in limbo,
My hair awry, my arms akimbo,
When I resort to electronic means,
And the rooftops ring with ugly scenes.

So, without resorting to more verse
Allow me to be extremely terse:
When in doubt, don't muck about.
Pick up a pen, and then
You'll doubtless hear from me again.

P Elias

SUMS WITHOUT TOTAL

Once again we try to state
That mathematics have a quota
That life, tabulated and expended
Less, not mattering an iota.

Heaped, stacked and counter counted
With numbers to condone
The hapless seek some restitution
When they are alone

And how more alone are they
With matching bars and torture
A patent or a duplicate is yet
Very far from nature.

And what has the perfect precision
In this original order
And careless splendour there is
An equation reached but never for disorder.

The books carelessly kept in columns
Many of seized life and death to all
Showed gross profit in this exercise
Their credibility too tall

And never, never it is know were
Additions added on the high degrees
In torture revealed or sacrifice bravely
Beknown, for those down on their knees.

John Amsden

DECISIONS, DECISIONS

Calling to the lost all around me is a guiding light?
I'm in a twilight world where only the fool can see
What is and what is going to be.

Is it the end for you and me?
There is a fine line to be trodden here
Whether this or may be next year.

The autumn tints with the turning of the wheel
For one more or may be next year?
Who knows, who guesses, who chooses?

What light breaks upon mellow waters?
Then throw caution to the winds
The outside world is beckoning
Calling forever calling like a bugle call
To the lost resounding throughout time!

It's time for life's test to wholeheartedly accept my fate
For what is and will be
To cast it, upon the wings of storm.

Jonathan Covington

SCHOOL HOLIDAYS

Sweet days of summer
running about having fun with my brother
splashing around in a warm dirty stream
eating yummy sticky ice cream.

Flying a kite, riding a bike
eating candyfloss on a stick
hoping that last ride doesn't make us sick.

Climbing a green slimy tree
eating hot dogs for our tea.
Reading a book or three
summer sweet school holiday.
It's so fun to be alive and free.

A J Renyard

WHO IS SHE?
(The Book Of Ruth)

Who is she? Who is she?
This damsel oh so fair;
Who tramps o'er barren hillside,
Meagre poverty to share;
With old and cursed Naomi,
Her mother in the Lord,
To harvest time in Bethlehem,
Though scarce can they afford.

'Do not make me leave you'
Was her heart's earnest plea,
'For where you go will I go,
Oh let me stay with thee;
For where you stay will I stay,
Your people shall be mine,
And your God shall be my God,
There is no God but thine,'

'Who is she? Who is she?
This damsel oh so fair;
Who gleans amongst my barley,
My harvest for to share'.
'This damsel is from Moab,
May my lord Boaz know,
And she has left her homeland,
For she loves Naomi so'.

Then Boaz, how he loved her,
And Ruth, she loved him too;
And she was to discover
His love for her was true;
With love he did redeem her
To make her his young bride,
How highly he esteemed her,
This fair damsel at his side.

Irene Hart

WHERE?

I hate the dumb stupidity,
Inherent in our race,
That gives us the temerity,
To interfere with space,
It may not have occurred to you,
But we don't have a dearth,
Of monumental things to do,
To bring us joy on earth,
It's costing millions year on year,
On sending probes to Mars,
While we destroy our atmosphere,
With aerosols and cars,
Yes, countless millions laid away,
The power mad to please,
While masses die each single day,
From famine and disease,
Instead of finding remedies,
For pestilence and wars,
They're treading on priorities,
While reaching for the stars,
They've little knowledge yet of space,
Whatever they pretend,
And I would love to see their face,
If asked, where does it end?

Matthew L Burns

SLEEP DIVINE

The perfect gift that would make me sing
A sumptuous bed that does everything
Magazines in colour parade them bold
There's nothing they can't do so we are told
You're not just to lie there, stiff as a corpse
But press a button and a new posture is yours
It will lift your feet up, now not too much
Or the blood to your head will give you a flush
Knees can be bent to relieve those pains
But I'm not sure what this will gain
Now to your back that's more like it
It will transform your bones to athletes likeness
And when you need to sit up straight
Just press another button it's never too late
So as I ache and groan and moan
At my arthritis as I'm getting old
With painkillers that give me the sleep that I need
I'll dream of a bed that stops you going to seed.

Gillian Mullett

BALLAD TO ROBIN HOOD

John he was a false king,
He claimed the English throne.
King Richard he was fighting
Far away from home.

Now John he raised the taxes,
The poor, they could not pay,
So John sent out his soldiers
To take their homes away.

The people ran to the forests,
They lived on what they could.
A good man became their leader,
His name was Robin Hood.

Robin swore to right the wrongs,
Done to the poor and needy.
His aim to get back what was theirs
To take from the rich and greedy.

He formed a band of 'merry men',
All dressed in Lincoln green,
So when they hid amongst the trees,
Not one of them was seen.

Robin and his band of men,
Would look out for some prey.
Attack the rich and take their wealth,
Then send them on their way.

False John he had a sheriff,
A mean and cruel man.
His job to catch Robin Hood
By working out a plan.

To lure the lad to Nottingham,
The wicked sheriff thought,
On pretence of much gold and wealth,
Then Robin would be caught.

Good Robin was not stupid,
And went there in disguise,
He took the wealth and riches,
From right before their eyes.

Safely back inside his camp,
The wealth was fairly shared.
Now Robin's found in history,
As one who really cared.

Christine Brown

GONE AWAY?

Mother Nature has gone away, they said,
Just look, all the flowers and trees are dead,
There's only the evergreen raising its head.

I looked, and for sure there seemed nothing to see.
Were they right, all these doubters, in challenging me
To doubt God's word as to what was to be?

For it states very clearly, in Genesis 8,
That even if springtime is a bit late
There will be a harvest well worth the wait.

So be gone, all you scoffers who doubt His word,
It's clear to me that you've never heard
How He provides, even for the bird.

For under the soil things are moving, I know,
As the shoots and the seedlings begin to show
Despite the thin covering of frost and snow.

Once again we are seeing, even through growth,
That the Lord can be trusted in His oath.
To let us down He would be loath.

That's good enough for me, my friend,
On Him I'm sure I can depend,
Until eternity shall end.

Keith Allison

THE BALLAD OF MOONSHINE VALLEY

The miners were waiting to do their shift
Conversation was high, all knew the drift
It was Harry Martyn that amazed them all
'There is rum goings on at Maddington Hall!'

Great excitement filled the night shift lads
Most of them being uncles and dads
They hardly could wait for the day shift men
Some asked, 'What's it like down there in the den.'

On went the light of each miner in the den
Young Pat Wentworth, he made for the tunnel whilst other men
Took their axe and worked on the seams
Their torches shining at full beams

The night shift over, the miners came up to the surface
Home for a wash and meal then, up to the Hall for the yearly race
Down Moonshine Valley to Adam's Beck
All wanted to win, the handsome cheque.

Lord Maddington stood on the steps of his Hall
He spoke loud and clear, 'I have my back to the wall
No cheque can I give this year one and all.'
'It don't pay to be rich, you're far better be poor',
Whispered young Tommy Ball.

Alma Montgomery Frank

THE BALLAD OF ALFERD PACKER

If you come to Colorado, where the mountains touch the sky.
Where the universe surrounds you, where the colours blank the eye.
Where the ghosts of myriad searchers tread their restless troubled way.
Then take a care for Alferd, as he stalks your soul today.

He began in Allhegeny, it was eighteen forty-two.
His parents named him Alfred and, as normal children do
He soon blossomed to adulthood, then he joined the Union Cause
In Winnona, Minnesota, but . . . the army found his flaws.

They labelled him disabled, they sent him on his way,
So he left the 'goddammed outfit', and early in the day,
He headed into Utah, and these omens should be told,
How he longed to guide prospectors, how he burned inside for gold.

It was early in November of eighteen seventy-three
Packer left from Bingham Canyon, where he'd agreed to be
A guide to gold prospectors in the Rocky Mountains range.
But as Alferd viewed his charges something evil augured strange!

They journeyed to the Rockies where the season settled cold.
In those cataclysmic canyons they began their search for gold.
But the wind was blowing bitter, while the snow was drifting deep.
And the lack of food and fire made their misery complete.

Then five of Alferd's party asked him to take them on -
Will Bell, George Noon, Frank Miller, Jim Humphrey, Israel Swann.
Did Alferd like the look of them? Was his unseemly haste,
To set them on their journey because he wondered how they'd taste?

And now events are clouded, and the truth is not too clear.
For Alferd changed his story and we cannot prove it here.
But we know he left the base camp with the motley crew of five.
And we know he later ate them, and we know he stayed alive.

In the depths of Utah's winter, when the wind is blowing cold.
When the evening light is eerie, and the shadows stark and bold.
If you spare a thought for Alferd, if you listen through the trees.
You may hear the sound of screaming, being carried on the breeze.

There's a moral in this story, for all who search for gold.
Be careful whom you travel with, beware the icy cold.
For in certain stark conditions, when they sense death's coming chill.
The nicest men go crazy - the gentlest folk may kill.

Now, as we think of Alferd, of the differing tales he told.
Of the years he spent in prisons, of mamon's iron hold
On him - It's clear that he was hungry and killed the 'famous five'.
Was it because he liked the taste, or just to stay alive?

If you come to Colorado, where the mountains touch the sky.
Where the universe surrounds you, where the colours catch the eye.
Where the souls of long dead searchers tread their weary tortured way.
Beware, beware of Alferd, for he wants your soul today.

Ray Smart

TODAY
(A Villanelle)

When Life seems but a summer day,
    And pleasure still on pleasure lies,
Then Time will hasten it away.

That love and gladness will not stay
    Is not in Youth to realise,
When Life seems but a summer day.

But when with sadness Life is grey,
    And hurt lies deep in youthful eyes,
Then Time will hasten it away,
For sorrow bringing sunshine gay,
    And letting youthful spirits rise,
When Life seems but a summer day.

But when one sees that in Today
    Lies happiness and growing wise,
Then Time will hasten it away
And let Tomorrow have its say.
    The Future on the Past relies,
When Life seems - but a summer day.

Then Time will hasten it away.

Mabel Helen Underwood

INDIAN WEDDING

A kaleidoscope of colours all around,
Sea green, red, purple, silver, blue.
Hypnotic music, bare feet move on ground.

My senses tingle, sight, taste, touch and sound,
I'm drawn into the revelry, like you.
A kaleidoscope of colours all around.

The warmest welcome, by them, I have found,
Though this is not my culture, something new,
Hypnotic music, bare feet move on ground.

Food, drink and hospitality abound.
I find that I am swaying fro and to
A kaleidoscope of colours all around.

Children perform a show that will astound,
The older ones show small ones what to do,
Hypnotic music, bare feet move on ground.

By now my senses are completely drowned,
I've become one with these strangers it is true,
A kaleidoscope of colours all around
Hypnotic music, bare feet move on ground.

Joyce Walker

THE VERY BEST YET

I will always remember and never forget
That little things mean a lot
Today is the very best yet.

To be forgetful only causes upset
In my hanky I have tied a knot
I will always remember and never forget.

I love to think of the moment we met
Our 'bumpers kissed' in the parking lot
Today is the very best yet

The walks we took during sunset
Dips in the sea when we were hot
Today is the very best yet.

I said 'will you marry me', your answer 'you bet'
So off I hurry, be late I must not
Today is the very best yet.

I am about to do something I'll never regret
To say 'I do' at noon on the dot
I will always remember and never forget
Today is the very best yet.

Sally Anne Hayes

WAITING

The house is perfect, garden neat,
white wicker fence with plants in place,
starched curtains stiffened pleat on pleat

Pristine as unused garden seat.
The garage closed - an empty face,
the house is perfect, garden neat.

No weeds or crumbs for birds to eat,
each bush in regimented space,
starched curtains stiffened pleat on pleat.

Two cars stand empty in the street
glowing unsullied in each case,
the house is perfect, garden neat.

No excess or extensive heat
wilts the image of 'don't touch' lace,
starched curtains stiffened pleat on pleat.

No sign of dust on each clean sheet
or squeezing of a child's embrace.
The house is perfect, garden neat,
starched curtains stiffened pleat on pleat.

Pam Redmond

OBSESSION

The years have not dulled my obsession
It still burns hot and bright
My love knows no discretion

My pounding heart needs some expression
Of this I must write
The years have not dulled my obsession

This must serve as my confession
My passion screams toward new height
My love knows no discretion

I am ecstatic in love's possession
My spirit soars free and light
The years have not dulled my obsession

I need no abstract frills to freshen
My soul is in full flight
My love knows no discretion

No matter our lifestyle or profession
A simple pleasure to hold you in my sight
The years have not dulled my obsession
My love knows no discretion.

Hilary Dominy

SUDDEN PAIN

Pain like a lightning stroke sears body and mind.
Wincing, aghast, frail nature shrinks away.
May I, in retrospect, some guidance find?

The whole of life to agony consigned -
It seems there is no potion to allay
Pain, which like lightning stroke sears body and mind.

No warning given to which I have been blind,
Nothing to tell to this, my ageing clay,
If I, in retrospect, may guidance find.

It seemed the depth of anguish I had mined,
Yet, ambulance-borne, gold gorse gave rich display,
Though pain like lightning stroke seared body and mind.

So strange, the following days which, undefined,
Escape my memory and do not stay;
May I, in retrospect, some guidance find?

If, this being past, I find myself resigned
To knowledge, that as life pursues its way
Pain, like a lightning stroke scars body and mind,
May I, in retrospect, at last some guidance find?

Kathleen M Hatton

THE RISEN SUNLIGHT

The road is rough with a dark glow,
There lies the risen sunlight that hangs between,
The surface of the evening wind below.

Raindrops that came with ripen fruitfulness,
Came flowers from the masturbating sun;
Concealing the love with harvest gratefulness.

Along the mountain with sharpened stones,
Lies the goat sheltering under the canopy below,
The surface of gathered bones.

Among the lillies the dawn awakens,
With misty dewdrop on the crop;
Which massages to the roots that we forsaken.

Farmers in bright summer frocks
Watch in awe at their embrace
To see the shepherds with their flocks.

The natives baked in lubricating sheen,
There lies the twilight of the evening rain,
With awesome fruits that lovers seen,
That catches the eyes of the village brain.

Dalsie Mullings

So Happy

I am so happy I could cry,
Because finding you seems unreal,
But without your love I would die.

For everyday I feel high,
Knowing your words of love are real,
I am so happy I could cry.

Reach out my arms to touch the sky,
With lingering kiss, love we seal,
But without your love I would die.

While beside you, think I can fly,
Surprise me with dreams you conceal,
I am so happy I could cry.

When you leave I give a huge sigh,
Waiting for more moments to steal,
But without your love I would die.

To be together we must try,
Side by side, that would be ideal,
I am so happy I could cry,
But without your love I would die.

S Mullinger

SEAGOING VILLANELLE!

We can't be expecting a gale?
The weather's so calm and serene!
Tomorrow, I'll go for a sail.

The barometer reads off the scale!
And the waves are much worse than they've been!
We can't be expecting a gale?

From my boat, all the water I'll bale,
And the tides are the highest I've seen!
Tomorrow, I'll go for a sail.

From the lighthouse I'm hearing a wail!
And I'm watching the wind - intervene!
We can't be expecting a gale?

As a Mariner, I must not fail!
Lest in public my fears may be seen!
Tomorrow, I'll go for a sail.

Fearful thoughts can a man turn pale!
Lesser men, might be turning - quite green!
We can't be expecting a gale?
Tomorrow - I'll go for a sail!

R Bissett

REFLECTIONS

This cannot be me
The mirror must be lying
Or is it very plain to see?

Must I agree
Could it be my looks are dying?
This cannot be me

Let it be,
Though years are flying,
Or is it very plain to see?

I do not want to see,
Perhaps the truth I'm hiding.
This cannot be me.

So I will no longer flee,
Just pretend I am not minding,
Or is it very plain to see?

But as I am now 93
Who cares at what I'm finding?
This cannot be me
Or is it very plain to see?

Winifred Lund

BROKEN HEART

How come time has not yet healed
my jagged broken heart
the knife still turns congealed . . .

My life with edges now revealed
will never be the same
how come time has not yet healed . . ?

Trust no longer can be filled
its grinding now subdued
the knife still turns congealed . . .

Hope has nothing left to heald
the loom has passed its yield
how come time has not yet healed . . ?

Succumbed entirely as is willed
to a life just left to fate
the knife still turns congealed . . .

Year in, year out, it has revealed
my destiny was sealed
how come time has still not killed
the knife that stays congealed . . ?

Margarette L Damsell

LOVE?

Love tears my heart relentlessly.
This my epitaph of hope?
So engulfed by my dependency.

I wait for you so patiently.
Freedom is given no scope.
Love tears my heart relentlessly.

I struggle but cannot break free.
I am bound by invisible rope;
So engulfed by my dependency.

Yearning for you passionately,
Scaling this treacherous slope;
Love tears my heart relentlessly.

A gentle caress received gratefully,
While my spirit you vulgarly grope;
So engulfed by my dependency.

Seeking confidence in my ability,
I strive to gain the strength to cope.
Love tears my heart relentlessly.
So engulfed by my dependency.

Marie O'Driscoll

RAG MAN

'Any old rags', calls a voice from afar,
Cartwheels rattle, hooves clip-clopping,
Visions of gold swimming round in a jar.

Through green latched gate with splintered bar,
Brown paper carriers stuffed with old stocking,
'Any old rags', calls a voice from afar.

Cool clear water bright as a star,
Fins edged with sunlight, turning, flopping,
Visions of gold swimming round in a jar.

Sound of whip cracking, joy to mar,
Cartwheels roll, no way of stopping,
'Any old rags', calls a voice from afar.

Into the distance, by St Ives Spa,
Dreams disappear, dusty cart rocking,
Visions of gold swimming round in a jar.

Treasure left steaming out on the tar,
Men with shovels, lads shouting, mocking,
'Any old rags', calls a voice from afar,
Visions of gold swimming round in a jar.

Joan Egan

To Stand and Stare

I'll stand and stare, since time steals all away;
The dazzling day a fleeting dream of light.
High noon's hot air foretells the end of May . . .

A dream of light; an isle, a gleaming bay,
Green shores, deep forests, mountain-summits white.
I'll stand and stare before day fades away.

There was pearled dew that cool in valleys lay,
Swirling thin mist over the waters bright
Reflecting silver star-like flowers of May.

As with the dew those flowers will never stay;
Roses will open green buds curled up tight;
Soon unfurled petals on winds whirled away.

Soft breezes blow over gold sands pale spray;
Waves from great oceans climb their final height,
Break in dissolving foam white as the may.

I'll watch all beauty passing like brief day.
I'll praise the Lord for all this rainbowed light,
These wild green springs with the sweet flowers of May,
And love all things the more that pass away.

Diana Momber

GREEN SHOOTS

Such small green shoots piercing the ground,
What hidden strength in one so young!
New life, erupting from that mound.

Forever upward, without sound,
Firstly a leaf, a bud, a tongue,
Such small green shoots piercing the ground.

Cold winter wind does not confound,
Now spring's clarion call has rung,
New life, erupting from that mound.

Ignoring feet, which by it pound,
How can it breathe without a lung?
Such small green shoots piercing the ground.

But from somewhere its strength it's found,
And its sweet song, briefly, is sung.
New life, erupting from that mound.

Before ere long, it will be crowned
With colours rich, bejewelled behung.
Such small green shoots piercing the ground,
New life, erupting from that mound.

Joyce Hockley

PIT CLOSURE

The wheels are still, the valley hushed and grey
No more will men be working underground;
The old remain, the young have gone away.

There is no reason now for them to stay,
The mine has closed and no jobs to be found;
The wheels are still, the valley hushed and grey.

Once there was hope but that was yesterday;
Once there was singing, now there is no sound
The old remain, the young have gone away.

With pride the miners suffered for their pay,
But now their pride within the pit lies drowned;
The wheels are still, the valley hushed and grey.

The slag-heap was a mountain built to stay
Now it has dwindled to a little mound;
The old remain, the young have gone away.

Now old men stare with eyes that seem to say:
'We have no life, though life was all around',
The wheels are still, the valley hushed and grey,
The old remain, the young have gone away.

Colin Palfrey

SENTENCE

Oh! With something more than prose:
Our laughter, from peppered stairways
With incantation, rose.

Our stifling; the swallowing hard of those.
The bugle call of days . . .
Oh! With something more than prose.

Our sentences; stubborn, stifled, choked: Goes
Where tears and sad-acting out of plays
With incantation, rose.

We played and lost and won - God knows!
And dumb-stricken, forged our ways:
Oh! With something more than prose.

Walked wordlessly, through nameless, numbered droves:
The essays . . .
With incantation, rose.

Of scurrilous, damned-sorrowing, divinely stretched: Who knows?
Pinioned in a phrase:
Oh! With something more than prose
With incantation, rose.

P J Harris

AS WATCHER LONGS

As watcher longs for loving's show,
Flow this to render repair.
And now, at last, will lovers know.

When, I beat, will heart's blood flow?
At Heaven's gate? Stand and stare
As watcher longs for loving's show.

Tread it soft on mountain's snow.
Gods are often distracted there;
And now, at last, will lovers know.

Lovers clash when fortunes grow,
Yet captured will they swear,
As watcher longs for loving's show.

Sands are quick, but sperm is slow,
Deceiving not to care.
And now, at last, will lovers know.

Grant me light in loving's glow,
Converting winds to air,
As watcher longs for loving's show.
And now, at last, will lovers know.

S Pete Robson

COMMUNICATION IS A MUST

Communication is a must,
Express what's in your heart and mind,
To those you love, to those you trust.

Explain your thoughts clear out the dust,
It takes effort you will find,
Communication is a must.

Release emotions your own disgust,
The loves, the joys that your heart bind,
To those you love, to those you trust.

It's up to you to make or bust,
Be realistic please not blind,
Communication is a must.

It will only take one large thrust,
Take one deep breath, speak and be kind,
To those who love to those who trust.

Your eyes will sparkle like stardust,
Loved ones have no axe to grind, yes,
Communication is a must,
To those who love, to those who trust.

Barbara Jermyn

DENY IT?

When you said for me your love can't die
You said forever true
How could I have know it was a cunning lie?

When you said we'll dream above the sky
You said a perfect view
How could I have known that was just too high?

When you said our love a knot we'll tie
I wanted that too
How could I have known your words would die?

When you said, yes you and I
More and more I loved you
How could I have known my heart to pierce you'd try?

When you said, it has to be goodbye
All my hopes turned blue
How could I have known the reason why?

How could I have known it was all a lie?
A love exists that's warm and true
I've taken flight and now I'll fly
One thing I'll say and that's goodbye.

Deborah Montague

WINTER WHITE

Crisp and crackling, winter white!
Snow falling overnight!
Houses patterned by the dawn!
Sleeping people woke and spoke
And the second act of the play displayed.
And nature once again
Has changed our lives.
It doesn't talk, it doesn't plan,
It doesn't just consider man!
This beautiful, terrible world!
It's kind and warm, clear and cold,
It's very, very, very old!
Its plan? To confuse man?
So wrap up warm and understand
The snow that covers all the land
Is a wonderful, terrible, valuable gift!
You cannot wrap it, you cannot slap it!
It'll only change in its own time.
No matter what you do. It's rare!
It's white! It came down over night!
It's winter, so it's there!

Joan E Blissett

ALL IS GONE AWAY

The rose bloomed
Filling the air with perfume
Then it faded fast

The petals dropped
The wind blew them away
Then there was nothing

No rose, no perfume
Only the memory now
All is gone away.

June Clare

TWO HAIKU

Youth takes his courage
In his pencil case for the
Trauma of exams.

Waking in his drey
A squirrel scampers down his
Home tree for the spring.

Gillian Fisher

FAITH

The mountain path doesn't end
   where it disappears into the mist
but continues, although not seen.

Leslie Holgate

HAIKU

Storm clouds gather above
Raindrops fall pitter-patter
Clouds now lay on ground.

On earth sun shines
Grass comes on earth
Green fields on earth

The flickering shadows
Full moonlight forest treetops
I see bats in flight.

John Clarke

AUTUMN SEEDS

Autumn seeds fall down
Scatter on the waiting ground
Rising in the spring
Small, hopeful shoots of beauty
Fighting to match their makers.

Danny Coleman

NATURAL PLEASURE

Simple is my life,
The breeze is freshly blown here,
Easy is my joy,
Each drop of rain falls pure,
The sunlight paints a rainbow.

Kate Laity

ALONE IN THE CROWD

In the crowded city
Feeling solitude again.
Resting on a bench
A man was wearing headphones,
Eyes shut, blissfully dreaming.

Millicent Coleman

TIME

Plunge your two cupped hands
into this cool sweet fountain.
Fill them with water,
watch the shining drops fall back.
So with time - it will not stay.

Feel the fine dry sand,
sun-warmed, shifting in your grasp.
See it running down
through slightly parted fingers.
So with time - it will not wait.

To impassive time
one minute is one minute.
Yet it deceives us,
swift in days of happiness,
it drags slow feet in sorrow.

Time once paused for me.
I stood still among the trees,
listening to silence
rare and lovely, not one sound.
Time waited, I remember.

Margaret Ballard

GIBBERISH

Gibber, gabber, goo,
Gang, goo, ga, gae, ging, gabber,
Gibber, gabber, goo.

Sarah Eden (11)

DEPARTURE

Remitting tides ebb
Enfolding functional time
To calm restive seas.

As choirs harmonise,
Quiescent tombs enclose
That random harvest.

H D Hensman

HAIKU

O muddy puddle
icing over contra jour
moonlit lake doth seem.

My damp face caressed
by diamond necklaced cobwebs
through December woods.

Janet Miller

TANKA

Six years ago I planted a tree
To give privacy to both neighbour and me
No idea what was to follow
Now mature it holds a nest
With blackbirds eggs
You imagine the rest.

B Holmes

HAIKU

Roses in water
Petals falling gone forever
The fragrance remains.

The blank page beckons
Awaiting inspiration
Of meaningful words.

Cherry tree in bloom
Wondrous in all its beauty
Some curse the petals.

Terry Daley

FOUR SEASONS

Firstborn white flower
Breaking through the frozen earth
Hope of spring to come.

Lush fruits of summer
Earth's ripe cornucopia
Feeds and sustains us.

Red leaf of autumn
Separates from its life blood
Dies to preserve life.

Tree silhouetted
Stark sentinel of winter
Will soon be reborn.

God grants four seasons
Giving structure to nature
Cycle eternal.

Catriona Barville

NOWHERE COMPROMISING

Where headed feet,
Unadorned, of popular pride?
Nowhere compromising;
Near enough,
To understand, of sand dreams.

Rowland Warambwa

INEXPLICABLY ENTWINED

In a remote distant past,
Into fruition came a chain of events,
One ape took the initiative,
From lofty heights he had a vision,
Yet was unaware of any future consequence.

The blueprint of God's creation,
Holds the question and also the answer,
Life He breathed into man,
Upright stance built a bridge between species,
A new era for the ultimate victor.

Was it by God's will?
Man's future destiny was moulded and preordained,
Or a twist of fate?
With the elements playing a major role,
And climate change diversifying nature's abundant habitat.

From the garden of Eden they stepped,
On the edge of Africa they stood,
Our ancestors in innocence journeyed,
We became inexplicably entwined forever,
Thereafter planet Earth would become our heritage.

Darwin his theory of evolution,
A random sequence of consequences beyond control,
What was the motivating factor?
Why did man become a savage predator?
Who has more intelligence man or ape?

In a war ravaged land,
Where only gentle giants dare to sleep,
Bullets fly through the air,
Does the mountain gorilla dream of slaughter?
Knowing that he is wiser than man.

Ann G Wallace

TANKA

Love is, two eternities
Merging into one,
Fireworks exploding
Then fading away
Without regret.

Vicky Stevens

HAIKU: HITCHIN

You ask me: 'Do you
ever visit your old school?'
Yes; in my nightmares.

Richard George

THINKERS

The world at my feet
The elements; sun, wind, rain, snow
Freedom at my pace

Tom, friend, fends for himself
In his friendship, hunger, cowering, growling always
His tail tells his tale

No town ever our home
No country scene ever viewed at a stare
No U turns, onwards only

Happiness is a coveted entity
No fun if no friend to share
Friend walks at my speed

No language between the two
Not a language that's ever been printed
A mutual understanding, no language

I have never looked back
A civil man will respect his mutual
Just out of mutual respect.

Hugh Jackson

NATURE'S BALM

The flowers blooming,
Colourful, perfumed and gay,
Drooping spirits stir.

Birds all twittering,
Swallows soaring in the sky,
Lift the spirit high.

Water's tinkling music,
As the fountain gently plays,
Troubled spirits calm.

Nature's healing balm,
Restores those who dare to seek,
Pouring in her peace.

F L Brain

SWEET VISION - A TANKA SEQUENCE

She moved from Cardiff
up to Builty Wells in Brecon
around nineteen-ten,
and my dad wooed and wed her
because of her great beauty.

Her hair was silky,
and gold as ripening wheat;
while her eyes and lips
were cornflowers and poppies
that blossom in fair cornfields.

Her voice was soothing
as turtle doves' soft cooing
in warm summer's sun,
and no bogeyman bothered
when she crooned sweet lullabies.

She smelled of lilac
and sweet April violets
through all the seasons
and even puppies loved her
and ran to her eagerly.

But this sweet vision
is just imagination,
for my mother died
before I got to know her . . .
and my dad never told me!

Dan Pugh

STREET LAMP

A street lamp flickers.
Sunset-orange glare is born
As twilight silence
Soothes the moving traffic roar
And proves there is magic still.

Jonathan Goodwin

AN AUTUMN WIND

An autumn wind,
Droplet of rain on my face,
Sweet, dark memory.

A turning leaf blown
Into the path I must walk;
The time Time forgot.

Helen Marshall

INSPIRATION

With a blank page
Looking back at me,
As I hold the pad upon my knee
All inspirations vanished you see.
Alas - black - woe unto me.

Then I feel a poem coming on
And must write it down
Before it's gone.
Or I might forget it
And it will be gone - forever.

A E Ritzkowski

HEAT

The glowing sunshine
Warms up all the day
Tar melts on roads
Like a flowing black river.

C Griffiths

IN ALL IT LIES

Amongst compassion,
Lies a place of blissful peace,
Attainable, to open hearts.

Sid 'de' Knees

NATURE'S ARTIST

Daffodils
Growing against the grey stone wall
Yellow
Splashed against the grey slate
Trumpets
Heart of the star shaped flower
Stem
Green and straight in contrast
Beautiful
Yellow, green and grey merge
God
Painter of this artistic scene.

Sonia Riggs

TANKA

Why keep looking back
Overlooking present day?
Take the road ahead
For adventure and progress
To avoid later regrets.

Hilary Jill Robson

AWAKENING

Silent the dawn air.
Is earth poised on a storm's edge?
A breeze gathers pace
Scattering dewdrops, pauses.
In answer, a lone bird sings.

Patricia Batstone

HAIKU/TANKA

Holding a shiver
shimmer of body and wing
dip of summer sun.

Today, tomorrow,
binding sweetly together,
what is your measure?
From grapes ripened on the vine,
can mature the richest wine.

Glenna Welsh

COMELINESS AND CALM

Question
Listen to the countryside what can you hear?
Does the echoes of wildlife go on, no matter if we stand still
Even when tasks we encounter?

Answer
The beauty that we see is meliorated as time goes by
And although nature we seldom see, it's often heard
So it will still be there tomorrow as if by magic, it appears.

John P Evans

TANKA OF LIFE

Snowflakes fall earthward -
of what do they remind us?
They are like us all;
drifting beautifully along,
disappearing with no trace.

Martin Mooney

ARMISTICE, RESISTANCE ENDED (TANKA POEM)

In grey battlefield
Warrior wields trusty sword
Hoping foe will yield,
And so, they with one accord
Throw down each lance, pike and shield.

'Treat us well' they said,
This enemy of the king.
'Many of us fled.
Oh! The trouble war does bring
Better that we all were dead.'

'Nay, you can stand tall.'
Quiet were their captor's words,
'For you did not fall,
Soon you will be free as birds.
Do not think of death and pall.

Over the hill and dale
With great courage you have fought
Till the moon grows pale
And all fighting comes to nought.
Please! Partake of bread and ale.'

'God's blessings on you.
Now hostilities can cease,'
And with words so true
The foe made a sign of peace.
From then on, the friendship grew.

Loré Föst

COMMITMENT

Perspiration rises on the brow,

Tasks maybe, too much
But who will help? Down trodden

Never seek an answer, boldly go
Fate arrives soon, at setting sun.

Albert Boddison

FIRST SIGHT OF SNOW

The ground was of snow
Lukas loved to play and throw
Although it was cold

It was fun to know
What you could do in the snow
Lukas now did know.

M Barnes

TANKA

The answer to the riddle -
A riddle of profound prestige,
Cannot be so found
When we pump our minds to see:-
True vision comes from our ticker.

Could such a question
Lead us backward to plains past
When we need to look
Towards our own self-made raft
Drifting down river to new shores.

Some can stop two hands
But one so easy on the eye
Someone could never deny
Finds power more intense elsewhere
Leaving time stood still in awe.

When you came to me
Within my beautiful dream,
It was always unreal
But it was never what it seemed,
When you found me in my dream.

Choler left swelling within
Gives us powers to bear Loki
And ever change our face
At one single breeze's beckoning;
Rain falling with no warning.

Chris Hatherall

WHAT IS A TANKA?

You ask me
what a Tanka is?
I should have thought it clear.

A Tanka is a glass, or mug,
that holds a pint of beer.

Ken Price

CROSS

Blair's June promises
Blossom and then fade away
Like love-in-a-mist.

Peter Davies

SHADES OF LIFE

First breath in pastel
journey through primary hue
Lay down in ochre

Conceived with passion
lain in womb of liquid love
Delivered with pain

Nurtured by Mother
nature revels in adolescence
Daughter - Wife - Mother

Melancholy dreams
curtains close on pensive review
The children play on

First breath in pastel
journey through primary hue
Lay down in ochre.

Susan Seward

IN A NON-HOLDING PATTERN

I crash land in the airport of your heart
I taxi down the runway of your life
Emergency exit, so set apart
Stacked in formation to avoid the strife.

Chocs away, cabbage crates, ten thousand feet
Candlelight dinners, good food and red wine
Propellers roar the pulse of a heart beat
Aviation love is simply divine.

I thought that we'd meet in the terminal
Flying on hope when my fuel tanks are low
And caught in emotion perpetual
But I never thought that you wouldn't show

You don't love me, parachute if you like
Radar, air traffic controllers' on strike.

Francis McFaul

FIRST FLIGHT

He dared with magical dexterity
To fashion wings, enabling him to fly
Across the boundless regions of the sky
To demonstrate his ingenuity.

His purpose was to leave the isle of Crete
Where Minos held him captive in a tower,
For this king ruled with dictatorial power
And all the ports were guarded by his fleet.

Escape by air was Daedalus' only plan.
With feathered wings he flew across the sea,
And though his son was killed, this artisan
Had proved his aeronautic theory.
So, myth records, man's quest for flight began
And this would change the course of history.

Celia G Thomas

ENDING

The heavy hand of time is calling me
Across the years, where mem'ry stands supreme.
So I look back and all the things I see
Are but a vision blurred, a fading dream.

As I lie here and think about those years
Of childhood, when the heart was free from care,
My soul leaps up; it seems that all my fears
Are foolish thoughts, because the world is fair.

And then I think about the endless day
That lies ahead; the tears and all the pain.
My heart then aches as I can hear them say:
'It's only time, just time, just time,' again.

But when Time calleth me into Thy wake,
O Lord, I shall go gladly, for Thy sake.

Sheila E Harvey

SEASONS

In spring ached for bells of snowdrops are born
morning dew dampens luscious green leaves.
Yellow primroses enchant us on a spring morn
and swallows build nests in dusty barnyard eaves.

When summer came on a hot day in June
the fragrance of roses scented the breeze
a sunburst from the sun shyly blushed at noon
and flowers of the honeysuckle belong to the bees.

Autumn is of nuts and sweet almond trees
when crunchy leaves drift all over the land
rain coated, umbrella days are here it would seem
and smoky garden fires are lit by man's fair hand.

But winter is a time of sadness and silently waiting
its sunless days and darkness and a kind of hating.

Maureen Cassidy

WHISKY

It flows out of a bottle and is whisky by name
The amber nectar tempts my tastebuds right away
But five or six drams later it all tastes just the same
And my spinning head pleads that will do today.

Another half dozen and I find things hard to say
With my slurring speech I want the world to know
That tonight is here to enjoy, for tomorrow's another day
So I'll have another dram before I go.

One thing sends a shiver from my neck to my knees
When I'm happy and there's some left in my glass
It's the curse of the barmaid shouting, 'Time gentlemen please',
Yes, they soon learn the best way to harass.

My sadness turns to happiness for from within I know
I left the bottle empty hence the reason for my glow.

Robbie Innes

GOD LOVES TODAYS

God made the day with love and care
For everyone to live and share
He made the stars and moon for night
To shine for us and give us light
All this He gave to all who dwell
We should be grateful, live life well
Love one another every day
But now the todays seem full of changes
Think before it is too late
Life was made for loving and living
Not endless fighting, shooting and killing.

Roger Brooks

BALLAD OF POETRY WASTE

When I read some poetry
Such a trash is all I see.
A travesty of justice, such a crime
Not a single stanza has a rhyme.

At each line I have to stare
Not a patch of that John Clare.
Reams of paper, such a waste
Letter after letter done in haste.

Only third rate wasting I fear
Turn in your grave Edward Lear.
Price of postage is the cost
Talent of the real poet lost.

There's been great poets through the ages
Now just junk fill some pages.
Like a poet by royal appointment
Did his pen need urgent ointment.

No idea on a ballad
Like a dull and plain fruit salad.
No warmth, so very cold,
Not a patch on ballads of old.

Colin Allsop

COUNTRYSIDE CHURCH TREASURY

Ancient villages screen craftsmen's treasure,
Saxon farmers, Roman settlers made tracks.
Workers built stone churches with skilled pleasure,
Focal centre for faith, friendship, wisecracks.

At church threshold, babes are baptised and blessed.
In the chancel couples join loving hands;
That theirs shall be eternal love's grand quest,
Closely knit in pure espousal's strong bands.

Guilds for handwork, music and sportsmanship,
Each year with world service and worship crowned;
Outspread for those distressed, one fellowship,
Bounty, loving kindness for all around.

The church proclaims that death leads to Christ's throng,
Raptured welcome, glad hearts, triumphant song.

James Leonard Clough

COMMISSIONAIRE

In fact the mannequin who came to life
to fix the fallen price tag - your suit
can cost an arm, a leg, if not the planet
here - found no fun in unfair tariff.
The dreadlocked star who shopped with mistress, wife,
could see him dust the cuffs, adjust the jacket,
run the willing errand, empty the bucket.
This loyal model could sustain the high life,
could pull the handle (salamander brass),
to bid you well for what there is in store.
But as commissionaire, tipped into debt,
feet fluid filled, he stood behind the glass
to get to pay, polished as he wore
no bulging heart on sleeve, his welcomes muted.

John McPartlin

FOREVER YOUNG

Yes the perfect body is hard to find
So take the people with lonely hearts
Buy their bodies and use their parts
Some people might think I've lost my mind
But we don't need low lifes and slime
The perfect cure for my kidney stones
And my poor eyesight and ageing bones
Maybe I could live to the end of time

My beautiful body could be on show
Such beauty I would never be alone
With a little luck no one would ever know
My arms and legs were not my own
So now if only I could get the dough
Then never again would you hear me moan.

Paul O'Boyle

THE OLD THATCH

To walk from Springfield up to Cherry B,
In springtime all the world is there to see.
The moors and meadows lie beneath the sun,
Where cattle graze and sheep in field do run.

The dancing tree stands proud upon its ground,
With years of history its boughs surround.
Imagine all the tales of long ago,
Brought up to date by locals in the know.

Around the tree the dancers weaved at play,
'Til evening shadows sent them on their way.
But now just walkers passing to the moor,
May stop at hostelry's inviting door.

Our walk's finale is The Old Thatch Inn,
A priceless gem, to miss would be a sin.

John Cook

REFLECTIONS

What is this soul this spirit that is I?
That meets the wall and searches out each shelf
A looking glass the answer might imply
Reflecting all before, but not, itself

Why do the foolish think that they are wise?
Promote themselves at every layman's door
Then fall and lose respect before their eyes
Repeat mistakes of those who've gone before

Why do the wisest know that they are fools?
The more they count the smaller is the sum
And stirring at the work of nature's tools
Now stand in awe of what they have become

So could it be that it's always meant to be
That that of what we are, we cannot, see

Oliver Eadie

BOMBS AND BULLETS

Bombs and bullets and gunshot sounds
The conflict of war strikes its attacking blows
People injured, ruined homes
Raging anger all around
Dead bodies lying, shock and confound
Violence and revenge that festers and grows
Widespread hostility, suspicion of foes
Frightened people, scurrying on the ground

People who are of a different race
Many of whom are persecuted by far
Sad child crying, home misplaced
Aware of the conflict, that blights and mars
Mass of destruction, left behind without trace
Orphans of war, bear the emotional scars.

R E Humphrey

EDEN - CORNWALL 2001

Biomes bubbling from a quarry belly,
The cavity gouged out by china clay,
Greenhouse bubbles outwit technology,
The eighth wonder of the world on display!

Plants culled from all climes and brought together,
A living laboratory all can share,
Plants for food, fuel, some crops for fodder,
Growing side by side in the humid air.

Crescent-shaped terraces on gaping sides
Tell stories of plants past, present, future,
Land reclamation shows a nation's pride
While plants of the world flourish in nurture.

A man-made Eden so contrived today
Fails to compare with God's natural way!

Pat Heppel

NOW AND THEN

Communications cackle through our time
Circuits and chips in the palm of your hand
Eternity's clock meeting out its chime
The hourglass slowly emptying of sand

Modes and methods beyond reason of man
A web spun from the deceit of mankind
Complex in design yet simple in plan
Technologies wrought from extremes of mind

A net to catch the knowledge of our life
Truth and lies at the tips of our fingers
Freedom abused and chaos running rife
Religions breath condenses and lingers

What's done is done and you can't change the past
The future is coming and coming fast

Tom Sawyer

RETAINING WALL

Most things have changed; the grassy bank which rose
In ragged shrubbery towards the park
Is bedded out in flowers and the stark
Facades of sombre mills no more impose
Their dismal presence, warring with the sun.
The setted road has evened to a tar -
Macadamed swathe, unblemished by the scar
Of tramrails and the pavements too have undergone
A change. Only the wall remains
To stir emotions and encapsulate
Dear echoes of the past which, covert, wait
For gleaning like Golconda's golden veins.
And as I listen I can still recall
Your gentle footsteps echoing by the wall.

Walter Blacklaw

THE EXILE

Empty and fragile and blown with the wind.
Allowing the breeze to tangle my hair.
An outcast from human contact and friends.
Exiled! Alone! Does anyone care?

A moment before in a hub of activity,
Pulled by the flow of passions and dreams.
Knowing the love of a familiar society,
Not knowing that then was not all that it seemed.

Deep rooted, the feeling of caring and coping,
Not taught to know the fickleness. Who can?
Dashed in a moment the dreaming and hoping.
Now standing alone! Discarded by man!

All this because you stood up for the cause
And condemned the falseness of sedentary laws.

Joan E Blissett

HIS LOVE

His love, she is no red, red rose, nor yet
Is she as fair as blossom in the spring,
Youth gone, now in middle-age she is set;
Nevermore to be a beauteous thing.
Her teeth like the stars, come out with the night,
And in 'Steradent' sit, gently bubbling.
Her varicose veins are a frightful sight,
Her ankle joints are ever troubling.
She bemoans the fact that her health is shot,
As coughing, she lights one more cigarette;
Overweight by far, slender she is not,
About small things will she worry and fret.

Though for her old age will come far too soon,
My husband loves this fat, wrinkled old prune!

F R Pavitt

WONDERS OF THE WORLD

True love is so pure
That when dreams are dashed
It will find a cure
A bandage covering where you've been slashed

When you don't know which way to turn
Which horizon to seek
Love can shine, simmer and burn
Until you are speechless, unable to speak

Love will take your hand, guiding you through mist
Climbing the ups and downs of rocky mountains
Through life's blows which hit you with a mighty fist
Guiding your dreams pure and as clear as mystical fountains

Find love and experience it first hand
It's a roller-coaster ride
Everybody needs it in each land
Someone to cherish, care and to be by your side

Claire Victoria Hale

WHO'S THERE?

Who tries to understand the way she feels?
When grief is hid and pain expertly masked,
And evidence of violence is concealed,
With persecutor never brought to task.

Who knows how many tears she sheds each day;
Within the prison walls she calls her home?
Would anyone believe her, anyway?
If she, her silence broke, and truth were told.

Who hears her frantic cries, within the night?
Or sees the look of fear upon her face;
Each time her pleas for mercy are denied
And yet another loathsome act takes place!

Who can she turn to in her hour of need?
But him, the perpetrator of the deed!

Sandra Wolfe

SONNET FOR MARIE
(Dedicated to Marie Hegarty, friend)

Here is Marie, beautiful, golden flame,
Of happiness, called friendship and gladness.
Burning joy in Eternity: I confess,
I looked to you for comfort, leaving the pain
Of my sorrowful heart and head. My rain
Upon your friendly shoulder, to address
My fears: you wiped away my excess
Of tears, for lost love: I bless to fame
Your heart and soul, for that moment you spoke;
'You hold grief for lost love.' I could not see:
My love is blind in love: tragedy awoke:
Samantha, does not love, old loner, me:
From those depths, my broken heart I thank you,
Marie, in friendship, you made my soul ring true.

Edmund Saint George Mooney

THE PLEASURE BEACH

We met each other walking on the beach,
When we were both morose and all forlorn;
When grief was near and love seemed out of reach,
Our broken hearts were stuffed with rags all worn.

We climbed each golden step of quivered sand,
And fled our pitch-black cells of misery;
Then walked together slowly, hand in hand,
Two ebbing hearts had found eternity.

At last we saw the sun's bright scarlet beams,
And birds emerged with songs of hope and joy;
A futile sea had waves of great esteem,
The stars and moon at night no longer coy.

Feuds concerning fact and fiction ended,
That delightful day when our lips blended.

Martin Howard

FOOLS RUSH IN . . .

There are mysteries in our universe
Dark undertakings we don't understand
Shadows seeking out the simple soul
Brandishing a lethal fiery brand

'Tis wise not to underrate the unknown
For what is known is insufficient truth
The fool alone belittles the beyond
And only sees too late the searing tooth

Temptation is the enemy within
She hints a joy but hides the consequence
She seeks the weak and takes him by surprise
The fool most apt to think himself with sense

Yet wisdom is the premise it is said
That fools rush in where angels fear to tread

Cherry

FREEDOM

She looked at death in her beloved's face,
A horror stamping on her fearful heart.
She saw an empty corner in this place,
A murky mist came down to jump and start.

The cross upon the wall was very dark
And spoke in silent words, in ancient tones.
There was no comfort for her soul so stark,
Her faith long gone, for all she heard were moans.

But as she raised her eyes up to the skies,
She found once more she could not disbelieve.
The cross that held the perfect sacrifice
Did not now say that she would never grieve.

The heron flew above her, flapping wings.
She realised the freedom that death brings.

Judith Thomas

'ECSTASY' - WHY? (A SONNET)

Why do they name a drug that kills
After something that is great?
Disgusting, rotten murderous pills
Should be titled to Relate.
Sexual fulfilment is known as ecstasy,
So killer pills should have a name that shows that they are shit!
Perhaps I'm on a soap-box, that doesn't worry me.
So if these pills were renamed 'Death', it may deter a bit:
So take away a selling point and call a spade a spade,
And let's call crap a load of crap, and not use euphemisms,
Let's catch the evil buggers who have this poison made,
And also those who sell such crap, and put them all in prisons:
I'm not against the use of drugs when used to cure ills,
I'm just against the profiteer who don't care who he kills!
If you don't think this killer drug's as nasty as it gets,
Cast your mind back a little way, and think of Leah Betts!

Mick Nash

MAGPIE

Such a dapper fellow straight from the beauty parlour,
Shiny feathers striding and hopping
So purposefully across the garden.
If I was a lady magpie
I'd marry him straight away -
No messin -
Just fly off and
Start a nest.
Mmm . . . why are we always
So susceptible
To bright gaudy
Feathers
And grand displays . . .
Is this why my old man has a new Audi?

Caroline Kemp

NURSERY RHYMES
(WITH GRAVITY)

Ring-a-ring o'roses, sung with levity,
atishoo, atishoo down we would all fall.
If only we were not blessed by gravity,
Great holder of the Earth's distorted ball!

Beneath the wall where Humpty Dumpty sat
strolled a cat, looked at the king and bowed.
The king bowed back with gravity. Then: Splatt!
Eating up the dainty dish, the cat miaowed.

When the Duke of York marched ten thousand men
to the top, not one of them came down again.
Found cockle shells, silver bells, and then,
left with a bevy of pretty maids; how vain!

Poor Jack went up the hill, fell, broke his crown.
Nowadays what goes up may not fall back down!

Norma Meadows

THE PORTRAIT PAINTER

There is a sacred bond of Communion
Between the portrait painter and sitter.
This will make for an inspired union,
Leaving impressions that will decipher.

The hitherto hidden will be revealed
Painting session after painting session,
And little by little the once concealed
Will present itself for recognition.

It is always great joy in creation
To retrace and recreate God's steps
And with positive skilled elevation
To interpret the recognised concepts.

A sacred duty one's subject portrayed
On canvas God-given talents displayed.

M MacDonald-Murray

SONNET FOR MICHAEL

I have regrets; they come at dawn -
With bright light comes reality:
The wash, the dress, the endless yawn,
Work, discipline, banality.

It gets a grip, it takes a hold,
It does away with all the dreams.
When teeth are chattering in the cold
Life's raw; or so it seems.

But in my cosy bed at night
I can be surgeon, astronaut.
As boxer I win every fight,
Surmount each hurdle brought.

I can truly say 'tis my one regret
That to lead my life, I must leave my bed!

Ute Elliott

GOLDEN AFTERNOON

A flash of white barred wings passed suddenly,
As on a wall a chaffinch did alight,
Began a trilling sound so fervently,
Filling the air around with pure delight.

The haze of summer like a breath of gold,
In just a few hours managed to condense,
The afternoon with summer days of old,
Which lingered in the mind's experience.

Blooms spilling out beyond the garden space,
Joining wild flowers carelessly and free,
Spreading themselves to every wayward place,
Sharing advances from the prowling bee.

Internally recorded but seen live,
Helping imagination to survive.

Kathleen M Scatchard

ANCHOR BOOKS
SUBMISSIONS INVITED
SOMETHING FOR EVERYONE

ANCHOR BOOKS GEN - Any subject,
light-hearted clean fun, nothing unprintable
please.

THE OPPOSITE SEX - Have your say on the
opposite gender. Do they drive you mad or can
we co-exist in harmony?

THE NATURAL WORLD - Are we destroying
the world around us? What should we do to
preserve the beauty and the future of our planet -
you decide!

All poems no longer than 30 lines.
Always welcome! No fee!
Plus cash prizes to be won!

Mark your envelope (eg *The Natural World)*
And send to:
Anchor Books
Remus House, Coltsfoot Drive
Peterborough, PE2 9JX

**OVER £10,000 IN POETRY PRIZES
TO BE WON!**

Send an SAE for details on our New Year 2002
competition!